Welcome to Our Coloring Book

In this book, you will find exquisite fashion illustrations created by the final-year students of the Italian Elegance Fashion Institute. Each design reflects the creativity and skill of these talented aspiring designers, inspired by the grandeur of Italian high fashion.

We hope you enjoy coloring these luxurious evening gowns and feel inspired by the artistry and elegance that each page offers.

Happy coloring!

ITALIAN LUXURY FASHION
COLORING BOOK

Exciting and Trendy Fashion Coloring Pages for Girls, Kids, Teens, and Adult with Over 55 Fabulous Fashion Designs

Thank You for Coloring with Us!

We hope you enjoyed bringing to life these luxurious evening gowns inspired by the best Italian fashion designers. Your creativity and imagination make these pages truly special.

We would love to hear from you!

If you enjoyed this coloring book, please consider leaving a review. Your feedback is incredibly valuable to us and helps us continue to create beautiful and inspiring books for all to enjoy.

Thank you for your support and happy coloring!

Warm regards,

Italian Elegance Fashion Institute

www.ingramcontent.com/pod-product-compliance
Lightning Source LLC
Chambersburg PA
CBHW081552250726
48653CB00009B/3394